KANJI

JAPANESE CHARACTER

SHOGO OKETANI & LEZA LOWITZ

STONE BRIDGE PRESS | BERKELEY, CALIFORNIA

Published by
Stone Bridge Press
P.O. Box 8208
Berkeley, CA 94707
TEL 510-524-8732 • sbp@stonebridge.com • www.stonebridge.com

Portions of this book were originally published in 2003 by Stone Bridge Press as *Designing with Kanji: Japanese Character Motifs for Surface, Skin & Spirit* by Shogo Oketani and Leza Lowitz.

Kanji on front cover: Dream (*yume*, p. 134); on back cover: Appreciation, Gratitude (*kansha*, p. 54).

Cover and text design by Linda Ronan. Kanji examples on page 7 by H. E. Davey (www. senninfoundation.com).

First edition published, 2016.

First on-demand edition, 2023.

Printed in the United States of America.

ISBN 978-1-61172-032-7

CONTENTS

The Way of the Spirit   108

The Origin of Kanji

The word "kanji" is the Japanese pronunciation of the Chinese word *hanzi*, which means "Chinese ideogram." The ideograms for "kanji" are 漢字. The kanji 漢 means "the Han people" (the majority race in China), and 字 means "letters." The original meaning of "kanji" is thus "letters used by the Han people."

Kanji are currently the only extant ideographic characters used in the world. Kanji originated from hieroglyphics carved on animal bones and turtle shells during the Yin dynasty, around 1600 B.C. By the time of the fall of the Yin dynasty around 1000 B.C., many books, including the first Chinese poetry collection *Sihjing* (詩経), were being written with ideograms. The style of ideograms seen today was established in A.D. 200, although there have been many evolutions in meaning since then, along with a general trend toward simplifying the forms of the characters. Today, there are over thirty thousand kanji accepted for use in China. In Japan the number is much lower: some two thousand for everyday use in newspapers and ordinary reading matter and perhaps another several thousand to accommodate specialists, scholars, and historians.

Beauty and Meaning

Kanji are incredibly beautiful and creative. They represent meaning in a visually expressive way, often mirroring the shapes of the things they describe.

For example, the kanji for "hand" 手 and "eye" 目 both look like the things they represent. The five digits of the hand are reflected in the lines of the kanji for "hand," and the pupil and whites are represented in the kanji for "eye."

手: 𗕩 𧘇 𧘇 手 手　目: ⊙ 𐃸 ⊙ 目 目

Yet some kanji don't look at all like the thing they signify. Rather, they form a chain of meaning by association. Let's take the kanji 計 as an example. It means "to count." This kanji is made of 言, which means "to say," and 十, which means "ten." It literally means "to say numbers from one to ten," or simply, "to measure or count."

Some kanji can express both meaning and pronunciation and were created in cases where there were homonyms. For example, let's look at the following three kanji, which are pronounced *pi* or *bi* in Chinese.

皮 (*pi*): "skin"
彼 (*bi*): "that," or "distant" as in "that side"
疲 (*pi*): "tired"

At first glance, you can see that each of these three kanji contains the component 皮. This kanji by itself meant "to flay an animal": hence, "skin." In ancient Chinese the words for "skin," "that," and "tired" were homonyms; each was pronounced *pi* or *bi*. So different kanji needed to be created to distinguish their meanings.

The first kanji was 皮 or "skin." This kanji can stand alone. "That" or "distant" was then made by adding 彳, the component for "going": 彼.

"Tired" was made by adding the component for "illness": 疒. "That" and "tired" have no connection to "skin" or to each other, but because they shared the same Chinese pronunciation, they shared the same component 皮, which expresses the pronunciation *pi*.

The main component of a kanji, often used to assign it a place in a kanji dictionary, is called a "radical." In the examples above, the kanji for "that" is classified under the radical for "going," and the kanji for "tired" under the radical for "illness." There are countless such examples, making kanji fascinating and complex explorations of symbol and sound. By adding radicals to phonetic components, it was possible to use a limited number of pieces overall to create thousands and thousands of unique, meaningful kanji. You will also discover that a kanji's pronunciation—called its "reading"—is not fixed, but depends on the kanji's meaning and context as well as the language of the speaker, whether he or she is a Chinese person speaking one of many different Chinese dialects, a Korean, or a Japanese.

Onyomi/Kunyomi Readings and Sounds

It is generally thought that *hanzi* came to Japan at the end of the fourth century A.D. as part of Japan's increasing adoption of cultural and religious materials from China, but recent research indicates that *hanzi* may have been introduced into Japan as early as the first or second century A.D. The Japanese adapted Chinese characters (which they would call *kanji*) into their language, using the borrowed ideograms merely to indicate pronunciation, disregarding the original Chinese meanings.

As we mentioned above, kanji can have more than one reading, and in fact most do. What are called *onyomi* readings in Japan are pronunciations that approximate the original Chinese pronunciation and are often used when the kanji is part of a compound, that is, a word made up of more than one kanji character. What are called *kunyomi* readings are native Japanese readings, generally used when a kanji stands alone, either as a complete noun or as an adjective or verb stem. In many cases, the native Japanese word existed before there was a kanji to write it and was simply applied to the corresponding character when it was brought in from China.

Similarly, onyomi compounds are often non-native concepts imported from China in civil or religious documents. The difference is a bit like that between Anglo-Saxon words in English, which to our ears seem earthier and more direct, and "imported" Latinate words, which often sound a bit more academic or abstract.

Continuing our example from above, we know that each of the three kanji built on 皮 is pronounced *pi* or *bi* in Chinese. In Japan, the Chinese reading or onyomi of these kanji became *hi*, which was easier for Japanese to pronounce. But each symbol also has its own Japanese pronunciation or kunyomi:

皮 or "skin" is *kawa*
彼 or "that" is *kare*
疲 or "tired" is *tsukare(ru)*

Kanji are used for most verbs, adjectives, and nouns in Japanese. Unlike Chinese, however, the Japanese language can't be written in kanji alone. Also required are two syllable-based writing systems—a cursive *hiragana* and a more angular *katakana* script—each consisting of forty-six phonetic "letters." Hiragana is used to write various grammatical markers, verb and adjective endings, and sometimes adverbs and words whose kanji are no longer in common use. Hiragana are also used to indicate the correct reading and pronunciation of a kanji, especially in books for younger readers. Katakana are used for emphasis and to write foreign, scientific, and onomatopoeic words.

Due to historical divergence, Japanese kanji sometimes have different meanings from the same ideograms currently used in China. Also, in some cases, as with Japanese words like *samurai* and *rōnin* that represent native Japanese concepts and have no Chinese analog, there are no corresponding Chinese readings.

The Kanji Aesthetic

Most Japanese designers like to play with the Western alphabet, just as American and European designers are starting to experiment with kanji. There are many different styles of kanji to work with, each one unique and beautiful.

The original kanji style—a primitive, rounded, natural form first written on bone—is called *kōkotsu moji*. This style developed into a less primitive, more formal style called *kinbun*, which was carved on metal. When written on paper, these shapes evolved into more stylized forms. Many designers today adapt these styles to create an old-fashioned, back-to-nature feeling. A Japanese restaurant in a rustic wooden building specializing in seasonal foods served in handmade earthenware bowls will typeset its menus and signage in one of these more primitive kanji styles, just as organic, natural, and health-food products may use them on their packaging and advertising.

The first modern kanji style is known as *kaisho* and is a block-print style. As people began to draw calligraphy with brushes, they needed a writing style that flowed more smoothly with the brushstroke, so a cursive style developed. This was called *sōsho*. Although the old style of *sōsho* was created at the end of the second century A.D., a new style of *sōsho* was created in the seventh century to make it easier to write. By the mid-nineteenth century, *sōsho* was the most popular style of writing kanji in Japan.

3 forms of the kanji KI

KAISHO
(PRINTED)

GYŌSHO
(SEMICURSIVE)

SŌSHO
(CURSIVE)

When the fountain pen—good for hard, straight lines and not soft brush strokes—was introduced to Japan in the Meiji period (1868–1912) and European-style penmanship became fashionable, the writing style changed back to *kaisho* and has remained that way ever since. The *sōsho* style is now used mainly for calligraphy, but to many Western eyes, it is the form that "looks" most Asian or Japanese, because it is often seen on scrolls in karate and aikido training halls, on movie posters, on menus, and on decorative gift items and other familiar objects.

Many different kanji fonts are used in printed materials. The family of Minchō fonts is used for everyday print, like newspapers and magazines (with its hooklike serifs, Minchō has a bit of the feel of Times Roman, the most common English-language word processor font). The font style known as Gothic (sans serif, a bit like Helvetica) consists of bold, square kanji and is used for advertising and design, as is Pop, a modern, round design that is popular in print and billboard advertising. There are also specialized kanji fonts like Sumō Moji for sumo tournaments and Kantei-ryū for Kabuki theater playbills.

Using This Book

In this book we have included several dozen entries, basing our selections on kanji and kanji compounds we thought were interesting, as well as those commonly found in tattoos and on clothes, accessories, advertisements, greeting cards, and other designs. We've provided five different kanji styles for each entry to represent a different mood or style, from traditional to modern.

You can scan, sketch, or photocopy the kanji here to provide a template to follow should you wish to reproduce the kanji by hand. While many people study years to perfect their calligraphy, you can produce reasonably good kanji by following a few basic rules and procedures.

First, make sure each kanji is in the correct position before permanently committing it to paper or skin. Be especially careful that the elements of the kanji aren't reversed from right to left or placed upside down. (We can't count how many times we've seen museum catalogs or books on Japanese culture or Zen with the writing printed upside down!) Be sure to include all the lines (and be sure not to add any new ones!).

Stroke order is crucial. Although not visible to the untrained eye, the order in which the strokes of the kanji are written plays an important role in the overall feeling of the kanji; even a subtle deviation can throw the kanji off-balance. When Japanese is placed vertically on the page, it is read from top to bottom and, if there is more than one line, from right to left. When placed horizontally, it is read from left to right, just like English. The flexibility of kanji to be read either horizontally or vertically makes them aptly suited to being tattooed on various body parts; vertical kanji lines for tubular arms and legs, horizontal kanji lines for broader torsos, backs, and necks.

When writing individual kanji, you also work from left to right. Strokes are written from top to bottom. Horizontal lines are written first, then vertical lines. In general, make the first stroke the top left line. Then draw all the horizontal lines except the bottom line, and then the vertical lines. Finish with the bottom line and add any small accents. The only exception to this stroke order is when you draw box-shaped kanji like 口 or 国. In this case, write the left vertical line first, followed by the top horizontal line and finishing with the right vertical line; then draw the inner kanji and finally add the bottom line. For several books that explain more about writing kanji, see the Bibliography.

For each entry, we give some historical or etymological background, sometimes adding an unusual fact or an anecdote or literary allusion. We have shied away from more fanciful interpretations of the kanji symbols, focusing instead on the actual etymology and background of each kanji for historical accuracy. Pronunciations are provided for all main entries. A letter *o* or *u* with a mark above it (*ô*, *û*) indicates that the vowel is slightly extended in length when pronounced, as in the example above of *fûjin* ("Wind God," pronounced *fuujin*) vs. *fujin* ("wife").

Due to our own interests in martial arts, yoga, and Buddhism, we have included many terms from these realms, which are often quite illuminating and rich. There is something for everyone in the Way of the Warrior, the Way of the Heart, the Way of Nature, and the Way of the Spirit, the four broad themes we have used to organized the entries. Zodiac entries that correspond to birth years round out the selection.

Designing with Kanji

Here are just some of the things you can make using kanji in your designs and décor:

- birthday or New Year's cards decorated with the appropriate Zodiac character
- rubber stamps and embossings
- website logos
- tattoos
- watermarks on stationery
- pastry designs and frosting decorations
- postcards, greeting cards, and invitations
- jewelry, sculptures, and carvings
- curtain and tablecloth motifs
- wall hangings
- glaze finishes on pottery and dishware
- meditation and journal starters
- screensavers, banners, and emojis on your computer

❀ ❀ ❀

People are always fascinated by different cultures, and we continue to be awed by the wonderful ways in which East and West have mingled in culture, lifestyle, design, art, and aesthetics. We hope this book will enrich your own experience of kanji in art and design and help you bring your creative gifts to bear in fresh, new ways.

武者

勇気

抵抗

愛国心

義

THE WAY OF THE WARRIOR

武　武　武　武

者　者　者　者

The kanji compound *musha* means "samurai warrior." The first kanji 武 (*mu*) means "strength," "bravery," or "weaponry" and combines the two ideograms 戈 (*ka*: "halberd") and 止 (*shi*: "stop"); it literally means "to prevent a soldier's riot with the use of weapons." Modern research indicates that 止 is a simplified rendering of 歩 (*ho*: "walk"), where 武 symbolizes someone walking with a halberd. The second kanji 者 (*sha*) means "person." The title of director Akira Kurosawa's famous movie *Kagemusha* (影武者) means "Shadow Warrior"—a "body double" who pretends to be a samurai lord to prevent the assassination of the real lord, thus foiling the enemy.

WARRIOR   *MU-SHA*

侍　侍　侍　侍

The kanji 侍 (*samurai*) was originally read as *saburo*, which meant "to serve the upper class." 侍 is made up of イ, which symbolizes a person, and 寺, which first meant "public office" but later came to mean "temple." The literal meaning was "a person working for the upper class." In early times, the aristocracy held political power in Japan, and the samurai worked as its army and guardsmen. These highly skilled swordsmen and warriors were called *saburo-mon*, or "serving people." Later, this term evolved to *samurai*. After the tenth century, the samurai started to gain power. By the end of the twelfth century, the first samurai government or *bakufu* was established in Kamakura, south of present-day Tokyo. The samurai class held political as well as military power, and the *shōgun* had far greater power than the emperor. By the mid-nineteenth century, the *shōgun*—a member of the Tokugawa family—was in effect the ruler of Japan, governing from Edo (Tokyo), while the emperor resided hundreds of miles to the south in Kyoto. See also WARRIOR.

SAMURAI *SAMURAI*

義　義　義　義

The character 義 (*gi*) represents a central concept of Confucian thought. It means "right behavior or action." "Duty" is often translated into Japanese as 義務 (*gimu*), which means "action someone is obligated or bound to take," but 義務 has the nuance of action taken involuntarily. If we take only the first ideogram, 義 (*gi*), the meaning is closer to the English sense of "personal responsibility" or a person's duty to "do the right thing." 義 is made of two radicals: 羊 (*yô*), symbolizing a sheep, which the ancient Chinese saw as a symbol of beauty and passivity and often used as an offering, and 我 (*ga*) meaning "I." The literal meaning of *gi* is "My behavior is in keeping with the right way of action."

DUTY *GI*

正義　正義　正義　正義

The kanji 正 (*sei*) means "to be right" or "correct." 義 (*Gi*) means "right behavior or action." 正 is made of two parts, 一 (*ichi*: "one") and 止 (*shi*: "stop"). Originally this kanji meant "to choose one right thing and stick to it." Interestingly, one of modern Zen master Suzuki Roshi's definitions of enlightenment is "to see one thing through to the end." 正義 thus means "correct way of life." See also DUTY.

JUSTICE   *SEI-GI*

力　力　力　力

This ideogram, when used alone, is pronounced *chikara* and represents the strength and power of a man flexing his biceps. In the kanji compound meaning "sumo wrestler"— 力士 (*rikishi*)—力 (*riki*, another reading of this character) is combined with the ideogram 士 (*shi*) from *bushi* (noble-minded person).

STRENGTH   *CHIKARA*

抵　抵　抵　抵

抗　抗　抗　抗

Both ideograms in this kanji have the same meaning—"defending and rejecting." However, 抵 (*tei*) also means "hitting," and 抗 (*kō*) also means "competing." The left radical in both ideograms symbolizes "hand." The combination of these ideograms literally means "to defend by hitting with the hands."

RESISTANCE *TEI-KŌ*

反 (*Han*) means "anti-" and 核 (*kaku*) means nucleus, or nuclear. The magnitude 9 earthquake on March 11, 2011, caused a huge tsunami to crash onto the coast of northeastern Japan. The tsunami destabilized the Fukushima Daiichi Nuclear Plant and caused a catastrophic nuclear meltdown.

The public was misinformed of the dangers, and the scope of the disaster was minimized. Radiation leaked into the air, ground, water, and food supply. The public was outraged. Huge anti-nuclear demonstrations were held in Japan and all around the world. The rallying cry in Japan seen on posters and placards was "*Hankaku*" ("No Nukes!").

The first ideogram *han* in 反核 is composed of 厂 and 又. 厂 symbolizes a cliff. 又 is "hand." The original meaning of 反 was "to climb up a cliff." In ancient times, sacred places were located on cliffs. Ordinary people were not supposed to venture into the sacred arenas of the gods. Climbing up a cliff was considered a rebellious action, so 反 came to mean "rebellion," "against," or "anti-."

核 (*Kaku*) is made of 木 or "tree" and 亥. Originally 核 meant "hard seed" or "core" (of a fruit). It is now translated as "nucleus."

ANTI-NUKE, NO NUKES *HAN-KAKU*

勇　勇　勇　勇

気　気　気　気

勇 (*Yū*) means "to be courageous and brave."
Here the kanji 気 (*ki*) is used in the sense
of "emotion." 勇気 (*Yūki*) thus means "courageous emotion." *Yū* is composed of the
ideograms 力 (*chikara*), which means "power
and strength," and 甬 (*yō*), which symbolizes
the sound of a flower blossoming. See also
STRENGTH.

COURAGE *YŪ-KI*

忠 (*Chū*) means "sincerity" and "devotion." 誠 (*Sei*) means "truth-fulness" and "purity of heart." The combination of these ideograms means "to devote oneself with a pure heart." Note that 忠, a central concept of Confucianism, is made of two parts—心 (*kokoro*: "heart") and 中 (*chū*: "middle"). Here, the 中 component expresses the pronunciation *chū* and also means the true feeling deep in the center of the heart.

LOYALTY *CHŪ-SEI*

愛　国　心

愛 (*Ai*) means "love." 国 (*Koku*) means "country." 心 (*Shin*) means "heart-mind-soul." These ideograms together mean "love one's country with the heart," or "patriotism." Today, most Japanese don't like this term, because the government used it to stir up prowar sentiment during World War II. See also HEART, LOVE.

愛国心

PATRIOTISM *AI-KOKU-SHIN*

忍者

忍 (*Nin*) originally meant "to endure in the face of danger." 者 (*Ja*) means "person." 忍 is made of two parts; the upper part 刃 expresses the pronunciation *nin* and means "blade," and beneath is 心, or "heart" (thus the idea of surviving "even with a blade poised above the heart"). The native Japanese reading of 忍 is *shinobi*, and in this case the kanji has evolved to mean "to keep a secret" or "to hide oneself." In the twelfth century, ninja warriors were mountain people who worked as skilled spies for samurai. By the sixteenth century, they had become invaluable assassins, informants, and espionage agents employed by the warring feudal lords. Men, women, and even dogs were used as ninja warriors.

忍者

NINJA *NIN-JA*

武蔵　武蔵　武蔵　武蔵

Musashi is the name of the great seventeenth-century Japanese sword master Miyamoto Musashi, who wrote the seminal work on warrior strategy *The Book of Five Rings*. Born of humble origins and named Takezō, he decided to change his name when he became a samurai. At that time, the area currently known as Tokyo was called Musashi—using the ideograms 武蔵—so he took that as his name. 武 (*Mu*) means "strength," and its kunyomi pronunciation is *takeru* (which was close to his given name); the onyomi of 蔵 is *zō*.

MUSASHI   *MUSASHI*

羅　羅　羅　羅
生　生　生　生
門　門　門　門

This kanji compound became famous from Akira Kurosawa's movie (starring Toshiro Mifune) of the same title. It is the name of a gateway to Kyoto built at the end of the eighth century. The original name of this elaborate arch was 羅城門 (*rajōmon*), which means "outer castle gate." In the eleventh century, with the fall of the aristocracy, the gateway went to ruin. It was believed that demons lived there. The current form of the name came into use in the seventeenth century and now, thanks to the popularity of the film, suggests a world in which there are no absolute truths, only shifting perspectives.

羅
生
門

RASHŌMON   RA-SHŌ-MON

雷 神

雷 (*Rai*) means "thunder" and 神 (*jin*) means "god. The Thunder God derives from a Hindu deity integrated into Buddhism. In Japan this god has been drawn as a muscular demon or *oni* figure like the Wind God, but he has drums on his back and holds sticks in both hands. In Japan, parents warn their children, "If you sleep with your belly button showing, the Thunder God will steal it."

THUNDER GOD *RAI-JIN*

覚　覚　覚　覚
悟　悟　悟　悟

Both 覚 (*kaku*) and 悟 (*go*) have the same meaning—"to become aware," "to awaken," or "to attain spiritual enlightenment." Originally this kanji compound meant "to learn the truth by shedding evil desires." But it now means "having the strong determination to take action at the risk of one's own life."

DETERMINATION *KAKU-GO*

鉄 (*Tetsu*) means "iron." The radical 金 on the left side of *tetsu* (鉄) symbolizes "metal." 拳 (*Ken*) means "fist"; the lower part of the second kanji 拳 is 手, which symbolizes a hand with five fingers, and the upper part means "top" (the top of the hand is the "fist"). The Japanese pronunciation of 拳 (*ken*) evolved from the original Chinese pronunciation *quan* in Shaolin-Quan (少林拳), a martial practice that is considered the origin of all Asian combat arts. For obvious reasons, Japanese boxers like to use this term— "Iron Fist"—as a ring name.

IRON FIST *TEK-KEN*

想像

頑張れ

衆道

繋り

和

THE WAY OF THE HEART

This ideogram is said to represent the shape of the human heart; the short lines on either side of the center line symbolize the chambers and aorta. *Kokoro* can mean "middle," as in "the heart of things," but like its English counterpart, the word "heart" has so many nuances and deeper meanings—spirit, emotion, will, affection, kindness—that it's often considered untranslatable. Among its diverse usages, *kokoro* symbolizes the emotional appreciation of beauty, as in this *tanka* poem by Saigyō, the famous medieval Japanese poet, who wrote, *Kokoro naki minimo awareha shirarekeri, shigi tatsu sawano akino yugure:*

> Even my poor heart
> unable to appreciate beauty—
> is touched by the snipes
> flying out of the autumn sunset
> at the marsh.

HEART *KOKORO*

和 和 和 和

This character shows the element 口, which means "mouth," next to the element 禾, which expresses the old pronunciation of this ideogram, *kwa. Kwa* has the same meaning as 会 (*kai*), which means "to meet." Namely, "mouths (people) meet and harmonize." *Wa* is one of the most highly valued concepts in Japan, and it has long been central to the Japanese lifestyle of "harmony and consensus." The original meaning of this ideogram is "to respond," but it has other meanings, such as "to become soft," "quiet," "calm," or "joined." Shōtoku Taishi, the revered seventh-century Japanese statesman, considered harmony central to living a peaceful life, and in his famous Constitution of Seventeen Articles he stated, "和 (*Wa*) is what we should most respect."

HARMONY   *WA*

平 平 平 平
和 和 和 和

The ideogram 平 (*hei*) means "flat" and is composed of a combination of stylized forms of 于, which means "balanced energy," and 八, which means "energy that doesn't stagnate." 和 (*Wa*) means "harmony." *Heiwa* thus suggests that when opposing forces meet, they balance each other to create calmness and smooth movement. In modern Japan, each emperor's reign is given a name; the current imperial era is called 平成 (Heisei), using the same character 平 to denote the nation's hopes for a peaceful and smooth development. See also HARMONY.

PEACE *HEI-WA*

美　美　美　美

This ideogram has two parts. The upper part 羊 (*hitsuji*) means "sheep" and shows the face and horns, and the lower part 大 (*dai*) means "big" and shows a figure with outstretched arms and legs. Sheep were revered as peace-loving and gentle creatures and were used in sacred offerings. Over time, the meaning of this kanji evolved into a general notion of goodness, docility, and beauty. Those who exist in harmony with nature, keeping their innocence, are considered beautiful, mature beings.

BEAUTY *BI, UTSUKUSHI(I)*

感 謝　感 謝　感 謝　感 謝

感 *(Kan)* means "to feel." 謝 *(Sha)* means "to appreciate."

感 *(Kan)* is made of 咸 and 心 *(kokoro)*, or heart/mind. The 咸 symbolizes an axe and a pot. A recent interpretation is that the axe protects or guards sacred words in a pot. It is said that 感 originally meant "to respond to God." 謝 is made of 言 ("to say") and 射 ("to shoot an arrow"), although here it signifies the pronunciation *sha*. The original Chinese meaning of 謝 was "to leave" or "to resign." When people leave or resign from a position, they usually part with words of appreciation to those who have supported them. So the meaning of this ideogram became "appreciation" or "gratitude."

In Chinese, 謝謝 *(shie shie)*, "thank you," is composed of the character 謝 repeated twice.

APPRECIATION, GRATITUDE *KAN-SHA*

誠　　誠　　誠　　誠

This ideogram means "truth" but also "sincerity" or "truthful heart." The left side 言 means "say." The right side 成 expresses the onyomi pronunciation *sei* and means "result." This kanji originally meant "to state the truth about one's own actions." *Chūyo*, the ancient Chinese book on Confucianism, states: "誠 (Truth) is the main way of the universe, and having 誠 is the Way of humanity." In *Taboo*, Nagisa Oshima's film, the nineteenth-century samurai faction Shinsengumi that was defending the Tokugawa government used this ideogram as its fighting symbol.

TRUTH   *MAKOTO*

清　清　清　清

This ideogram originally represented a stream of clear water. The left part (the three "droplets") symbolizes water, and the right side represents the pronunciation *sei*. The kanji also means "blue," like the color of clear water. Kiyomizu-dera (**清水寺**), the famous temple on stilts in eastern Kyoto, uses this kanji in its name, a reference to the clear spring water flowing down from the mountain nearby.

CLARITY   *SEI*, *KIYO(I)*

情 情 情 情

The literal translation of this kanji is "hot emotion" or "emotional fever," since 情 (*jō*) means "emotion" and 熱 (*netsu*) means "fever" or "hot/heated." The upper part of 熱 symbolizes a burst of energy, and the four points below symbolize fire. As a whole, Japanese people are more known for their calm restraint than their hot-headed passion. Kabuki drama, however, provides many passionate characters. One of the most famous is O-Shichi, a sixteen-year-old girl who fell in love with a young priest at a temple where her family had taken refuge from a fire. After the family returned home, she couldn't get him out of her mind and finally set her house afire so that she could return to the temple. The fire was quickly put out, but O-Shichi was sentenced to death. In old Japan, where a single house on fire could destroy a whole town of paper-and-wood houses, arson was a serious crime.

PASSION   *JŌ-NETSU*

繋り　繋り　繋り　繋り

After the Great East Japan Earthquake of March 11, 2011, Japanese people began to use the word *tsunagari*, or "bond," to show support for those affected by the triple disaster of the earthquake, tsunami, and nuclear meltdown.

The ideogram 繋 contains the radical for "string," or 糸. The original Chinese meaning is "to tie together with rope" or "bind." In Japanese, the kanji contains the original Chinese meaning but also the meaning of bonding or connecting people. The expression *"Tsunagarō Nippon!"* or "Come Together, Japan" became popular after 3-11-11.

Another kanji, 絆 or *kizuna*, was also used to support Tohoku and appeared in many songs, manga, anime, and advertisements. Like *tsunagari*, it also means "bond" and contains the radical for string, 糸. *Kizuna* originally was for a thin, flat rope used to yoke animals to poles, but in the modern Japanese context 絆 has come to mean "a strong connection between people." (In modern Chinese, in contrast, 絆 means "to obstruct" or "to disturb." As is often case with kanji, each country has adapted the character according to its own culture and history.)

BOND   *TSUNAGARI*

福　福　福　福

The left side of this ideogram symbolizes the divine, and the right side expresses the Japanese pronunciation *fuku*. Pleasing the gods leads to happiness, both divine and human. At Shinto shrine harvest festivals you often see sacred Kagura dancers wearing the comical white mask of the rosy-cheeked woman Otafuku (**お多福**), whose name means "great happiness" and whose movements are intended to give the gods pleasure.

HAPPINESS   *FUKU*

優　優　優　優

This ideogram originally meant "spacious" but has evolved to mean "kind," "excellent," "good," "generous," and "able." Osamu Dazai, the popular "decadent" novelist who committed suicide in 1948, commented that this ideogram , made of two parts—イ symbolizing a person, and meaning "to feel sad and grieve"—in essence shows how a person who can feel sadness has a kind heart.

KINDNESS   YASASHI(I)

衆　衆　衆　衆
道　道　道　道

The kanji compound 衆道 is the old Japanese term for "homosexual." (There is no separate term for "lesbian.") Originally, homosexuality was called 若衆道 (*wakashūdō*), which means, roughly, "[following] the Way (道) of young boys (若衆)." Before westernization in the nineteenth century, homosexuality was not taboo in Japan but, as in ancient Greece, was embraced by the upper classes, particularly the samurai warriors. Bisexuality was in fact the norm for Japanese men from samurai to ordinary citizens. In the fourteenth century, Ashikaga Takauji, the first *shōgun* of the Muromachi government, formed a horseback battalion of his young male lovers, called the Hanaikki (花一揆), or "Flower Corps."

GAY   *SHŪ-DŌ*

独 (*Doku*) means "to be alone," and 立 (*ritsu*) means "to stand up." The literal meaning of this kanji is thus "to stand up by one-self" or "to stand on one's own." The original ideogram of 独 was 獨, but as this was too complex to write, the form was simplified. The radical on the left means "animal," and the character originally illustrated a pack of dogs biting each other. Later, the meaning evolved into its opposite; rather than "pack," it now means "alone."

INDEPENDENCE *DOKU-RITSU*

頑張れ 頑張れ 頑張れ 頑張れ

Ganbare is basically a call to action, an encouragement, a way to cheer someone up. It can be translated in any number of ways, including "Hang in there!" "Go for it!" "Do your best!" "Don't give up!" "You can do it!"

The verb *ganbaru* is of Japanese origin and is written by combining the kanji 頑 ("to be stubborn") and 張 ("to pull tightly"). After the Great East Japan Earthquake of 3-11-11, the expression 頑張ろう！東北 *Ganbarō! Tōhoku* (Hang in there, Tohoku!) was used to encourage those who had experienced the disaster and to let them know they were not alone.

頑張れ

GO FOR IT!　GAN-BARE

想　想　想　想

像　像　像　像

The first kanji 想 (*sō*) means "to think" or "to imagine." 像 (*Zō*) means "object" or "shape." This kanji literally means "to imagine a shape," but the original meaning of this term was "to imagine an elephant" (the radical on the right—象—means "elephant" and is pronounced *zô*). Elephants lived in southern China around 1500 B.C. when the kanji 象 was first created, but by 1000 B.C. these animals had completely perished and no one alive then had ever actually seen one. So when these later Chinese saw elephant bones brought in from Southeast Asia they could only imagine the shape of this enormous animal. That is how the kanji compound 想像 meaning "imagination" came to be made of the ideograms for "imagine" (想) and "the shape of an elephant" (象).

IMAGINATION   SŌ-ZŌ

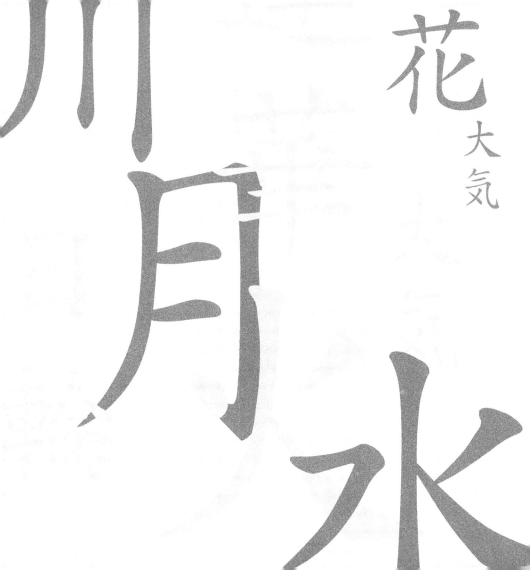

THE WAY OF NATURE

陰
陽

陰　陰　陰　陰
陽　陽　陽　陽

Nature and human nature dance between light and dark, sun and moon, male and female, day and night. The balance and embrace of opposite forces is at the heart of the Chinese view of the cosmos. The kanji for *in* (陰) represents a hill covered by a shelter or roof (今), symbolizing shade, coolness, and a negative charge. The kanji for *yō* (陽) represents a sunny, open space, symbolizing light, warmth, and a positive charge. Emptiness cannot exist without fullness, nor light without dark. *In* is considered feminine energy, and *yō* is considered masculine. In Chinese, these kanji are pronounced *yin yang*; the familiar symbol ☯ of complementary shapes and shades represents this concept of eternal balance.

IN / YŌ (DUAL FORCES OF NATURE)

大地　大地　大地　大地

The kanji 大 (*dai*) represents a person with arms and legs spread in an open posture of receptivity and means "big" or "great." *Chi* (地) means "land"; the radical 土 on the left indicates "soil," and the right part 也 is said to have originally symbolized a vagina. The great Earth Mother is revered in Japanese culture. The common Japanese translation of "Planet Earth" is *chikyū* (地球), but 大地 (*daichi*) is a less-scientific and more poetic-sounding term.

EARTH   *DAI-CHI*

大 大 大 大

気 気 気 気

The first kanji 大 (*tai*) means "big" or "great." 気 (*Ki*) represents the life-force energy within us (also called *qi* or *chi* in Chinese and *prana* in Sanskrit), but it also means "invisible power," "the meeting of earth and sky," and "breath." Here, 気 is used to mean "air"— the air that covers the entire earth; the form is a simplification of the original Chinese character 氣, which symbolized the steam rising from cooked rice. The common Japanese translation of "air" is *kūki* (空気), a more scientific term.

大気

AIR *TAI-KI*

水　水　水　水

This character symbolizes water flowing smoothly. To cultivate equanimity, we should allow the challenges of life to flow around us, like a river around rock. Lao-tzu said, "The highest good is like water. Water gives benefit to all beings in this world. It never fights. Furthermore, it is content to stay in a humble place."

WATER *MIZU*

火　火　火　火

This kanji represents a burning flame. Fire has long been revered by many ancient world cultures as a symbol of purification and renewal. Throughout Japan, fire ceremonies are sacred rituals held in shrines and temples to this day. One of the most famous is the Mt. Kurama Fire Festival, or Kurama no Hi Matsuri (鞍馬の火祭り), which is held annually in northern Kyoto on the night of October 22 and features people running through the mountains carrying hundreds of brightly lit torches to welcome the gods.

FIRE   *HI*

山　山　山　川

This kanji is in the shape of three peaks, symbolizing a mountain spreading the energy contained within it outward. Some 75 percent of Japan's land mass is mountainous, and since ancient times mountains in Japan were considered sacred bridges from this world to the spirit world. Legend has it that the massive mountain gods loved to practice sumo wrestling with each other.

MOUNTAIN   *YAMA*

川　　川　　川　　川

This ideogram symbolizes a stream or a river. Water flows swiftly down mountain streams, evoking the Buddhist concept of *mujō* (無常) or transience, that is, a state of constant change where nothing remains as it is from one moment to the next. Japan has its own version of Heraclitus' famous dictum "You can't step in the same river twice." The twelfth-century poet Kamo no Chōmei wrote, "The flowing river never stops and yet the water never stays the same."

RIVER *KAWA*

海　海　海　海

The three droplets on the left side of this character symbolize water, and the element on the right symbolizes grass growing
abundantly. The kanji thus represents a great and powerful flow
of water, like the vast ocean. The original ideogram for "ocean"
contained the character for mother, *haha* (母), in the lower right. In
French, the ocean is *la mer*, and mother is *la mère*. Tatsuji Miyoshi,
a modernist poet, wrote of this strange connection that cut across
language and cultures:

> Ocean, in the language we use
> there is a mother inside you
> And mother, in the language the French use
> there is an ocean inside you.

OCEAN   *UMI*

月　月　月　月

This kanji symbolizes a crescent shape. In Japanese, the full moon is called *jūgoya* (十五夜), which means "fifteenth night." The most beautiful moon of the year is said to be the full moon in September. On that night, people—especially poets and lovers—hold a moon-viewing ceremony called *tsukimi* (月見) and offer dumplings (and verse) to express gratitude to our celestial companion.

MOON   *TSUKI*

日輪　日輪　日輪　日輪

This kanji compound means "a round and shining sun." 日 (*Nichi*) symbolizes a shining sun and also means "day." *Rin* (輪) means "circle." The element 車 on the left of 輪 means "vehicle," and the element 侖 on the right represents a round shape and expresses the pronunciation *rin*. The customary Japanese word for "sun" is *taiyō* (太陽), but *nichirin* has a more classical, poetic sound.

日輪

SUN   *NICHI-RIN*

花　花　花　花

This kanji meaning "flower" is a combination of the symbols for "grass" (top) and "change" (bottom). The "change" element 化 also expresses the onyomi pronunciation *ka*. The fleeting beauty of the cherry blossom, which shines brightly for but a very short time before its petals fall or are swept away by the wind, embodies the idea of change and has come to symbolize Japanese aesthetic taste. The most beautiful cherry blossoms are on Mt. Yoshino in Nara Prefecture. Saigyō, the Japanese poet who lived in seclusion on Mt. Yoshino, wrote:

> I wish I could die under the full cherry blossoms
> on the full moon of February
> when Buddha entered Nirvana.

Saigyō in fact got his wish and died on February 16, 1190.

FLOWER *HANA*

This kanji contains 虫 (*mushi*), the ideogram for "insect," because the ancient Chinese believed it was the blowing wind that gave birth to insects. The Japanese consider wind one of the most beautiful of the four primary elements of nature—along with flowers, birds, and the moon—collectively referred to as *kachōfūgetsu* (花鳥風月). Bashō wrote often of the wind, as in this haiku:

> Mt. Arashi—
> inside the growing bush
> a stream of wind

WIND *FŪ, KAZE*

光　光　光　光

The upper part of this character, a stylized form of 火, symbolizes "fire," and the bottom part, a stylization of 人, represents a person, signifying "function." The function of fire is light. In Japan, the statues of Amitabha Buddha have a round glowing sphere behind him to symbolize the infinite light and life he radiates. In Japanese, a supreme being is *gokō ga sasu* (後光が差す) or "someone who shines with radiant light from behind."

LIGHT   *KŌ, HIKARI*

闇　闇　闇　闇

This ideogram is made of , which means "gate," and , which means "sound" but also expresses the onyomi pronunciation *an*. The gate symbolizes a closed-off place where only the faintest sounds of the world can be heard.

DARKNESS   *YAMI*

蓮 蓮 蓮 蓮
華 華 華 華

The kanji 蓮 (*ren*) means "the lotus" and 華 (*ge*) means "flower." In Buddhism, the lotus symbolizes the Pure Land of Heaven. This symbol came from the *Saddharmapundrika Sutra*. *Saddharma* means "the right laws of the universe." *Pundrika* refers to the lotus flower. Born in a muddy marsh, the lotus grows to enormous beauty and rises above its humble origins. Like it, humans can rise above their circumstances and transform their lives without being pulled into the swamp of earthly desires and suffering. In Japan, the *Lotus Sutra* is known as 妙法蓮華経 (*Myōhō renge kyō*).

LOTUS *REN-GE*

瑜伽

涅槃
仏性

愛

無

THE WAY OF THE SPIRIT

道　道　道　道

The right side 首 of this character is the kanji for "neck," which symbolizes the top of the head, the highest place in the body. It also means "goal." The trailing element on the left means "to go to." The ideogram 道 (*michi* in Japanese or *tao* in Chinese) means "the Way" or "the path," the central concept in Taoism. Lao-tzu interpreted the Tao as the basic law of the universe, saying, "道 (the Way) is like a vessel. Even when emptied over and over again, it doesn't need to be full. New water always springs forth, and it is bottomless. It is like the origin of everything." Many martial arts and artistic disciplines apply the kanji 道 (usually read *dō* when used in a compound) to their names to indicate that they are fundamentally concerned with spiritual growth: *aikidō*, *shodō* (calligraphy), *kadō* (flower arrangement), *sadō* (tea ceremony), and so on.

THE WAY *DŌ, MICHI*

無　無　無　無

The ideogram 無 (*mu*) represents a very profound Zen expression meaning "nothingness," "the void," and "the original cosmos beyond existence or nonexistence." In the ninth century, the Chinese priest Jōshū was asked the following Zen koan by another priest: "Does a dog have Buddha nature ()?" Jōshū's answer was "." In Buddhism, every being in this world has Buddha nature. Jōshū's answer essentially means, "When we reach the state of 無, it doesn't matter." See also BUDDHA NATURE.

NOTHINGNESS *MU*

菩薩　菩薩　菩薩　菩薩

The word "bodhisattva" comes from the Sanskrit word *bodhi*. A *bodhi* is someone who has undergone intense spiritual training to reach a state of enlightenment and who is committed to helping others alleviate suffering. Dharmakara Bodhisattva (法蔵菩薩), who later became Amitabha Buddha, is a familiar example. When he became a bodhisattva he vowed, "I cannot become a Buddha until all beings in this world are saved."

BODHISATTVA *BO-SATSU*

瑜　瑜　瑜　瑜
伽　伽　伽　伽

The kanji 瑜 means "a type of jade"; the element 王 on the left means "jewelry," and the radical on the right expresses the pronunciation *yu*. The kanji 伽 is used to express the Sanskrit pronunciation *ga* or *ka*. Yoga in Buddhism is different from the yoga that is currently practiced in most yoga studios, which emphasize postures, breathing, chanting, and meditation. In Buddhism, *yuga* is taking care of the mind, body, and spirit through *zazen*-style sitting, breathing, and meditation.

YOGA   *YU-GA*

解脱　解脱　解脱　解脱

The first character 解 means "unbind" and is made of the elements "horn" (角), "sword" (刀), and "ox" (牛). Its original meaning was "to cut the ox," that is, to separate the meat from the bone. The second character 脱 means "to cast off"; the radical on the left means "body," and that on the right means "separate." *Gedatsu*, a Buddhist term that means "to cut the binds of desire, worry, and suffering to attain enlightenment," is a translation of the Sanskrit *vimukti*, which means "total liberation." Rinzai, a ninth-century Zen priest, said, "When you meet the Buddha, kill the Buddha. When you meet your ancestors, kill your ancestors. When you meet an *arhat* [an enlightened monk], kill the *arhat*. Then, you will finally be liberated (解脱)."

解
脱

LIBERATION   *GE-DATSU*

空　空　空　空

The ideogram 空 (*kū*) means "emptiness" and is the Chinese translation of the Sanskrit term *sunyata* or "void." Its antonym is 色 (*shiki*), meaning "all that has form." 空 is made of "hole" (穴) and the element 工, which expresses the pronunciation *kū*. A famous phrase in the *Parajaparmita Sutra* says 色即是空 (*shiki soku ze kū*: "form is emptiness") and 空即是色 (*kū soku ze shiki*: "emptiness is form"). The kanji 空 can also be pronounced *kara*, as in the martial art 空手 (*karate*), whose literal meaning is "empty hand."

EMPTINESS *KŪ, KARA*

正業

The first kanji 正 (*shō*) means "good," "correct," or "just." The original meaning of the second kanji 業 (*gō*) is "skill" and "work," but when Buddhism came to China this kanji was used to translate the Sanskrit term *karma*, the past-life deeds or actions that are the determinants of one's current existence. On its own, the ideogram 業 for *karma* generally means "bad karma" in Japanese, since if our past life had been virtuous we would be in the Pure Land instead of being reborn into human form. Therefore, we combine the two ideograms to form 正業 (*shōgō*) or "good karma."

GOOD KARMA *SHŌ-GŌ*

涅槃　涅槃　涅槃　涅槃

The two ideograms 涅槃 represent the Sanskrit word *nirvana*. The original meaning of *nirvana* was "to blow off" the fire of earthly cravings, reaching an ideal state of complete freedom from desire, worry, and suffering. Someone who has reached *nirvana* breaks the cycle of *karma* and will no longer be incarnated in earthly form. Though the day Buddha reached *nirvana* is unknown, February 15 is honored as Buddha's death day. On that day, memorial ceremonies called *nehan-e* (涅槃会) are held in temples throughout Japan, Korea, and China. See also FLOWER.

涅槃

NIRVANA *NE-HAN*

禅　禅　禅　禅

The word "Zen" (禅) comes from the Buddhist term 禅那 (*zenna*), the Chinese pronunciation of the Sanskrit term *dhyana*, which means "concentration" as a means of awakening consciousness— one of the eight limbs of yogic practice as stated in the *Yoga Sutra*. Zen is widely known as a type of Buddhist practice in which meditation serves as the gateway to liberation. Zen came to Japan from China in the twelfth century and was the most popular religion of the samurai class in medieval times. It has profoundly influenced almost all Japanese artistic, martial, and spiritual practices.

ZEN   *ZEN*

仏 仏 仏 仏
性 性 性 性

The kanji compound 仏性 (*busshō*) represents the Sanskrit term *budhata*, which means "Buddha nature." The first kanji 仏 (*butsu*) means "the Buddha," and 性 (*shō*) means "nature" or "essence." *The Mahaparinibbanasuttanta*, the sacred Buddhist text that documents the days before and after the Buddha's death, quotes Buddha: "Every being in this world has Buddha nature." Even dogs, cats, insects, and plants have Buddha nature, the ability to attain enlightenment and to be awakened. The main concept of Buddhism, often overlooked, is that nirvana is available to all.

BUDDHA NATURE   *BUS-SHŌ*

鬼　　鬼　　鬼　　鬼

In China, the kanji 鬼 originally meant "soul" or "departed spirit," but in Japanese it symbolizes a muscle-bound demon with red or blue skin and two horns growing from its head. Japanese folklorists believe the term might have first been used to describe the indigenous Japanese people, or Emishi, who fought against the emperor's occupying army from the third to eighth centuries. The emperor's troops, who encountered the bitter resistance of the Emishi as they struggled to keep their land, called them *oni* or "demons." Nowadays, Japanese sometimes use 鬼 in a more positive way; for example, someone who works with near-inhuman energy is a 仕事の 鬼 (*shigoto no oni*: literally, a "demon worker"). See also Soul.

DEMON *KI, ONI*

魂　　魂　　魂　　魂

The right part of this ideogram contains 鬼 (*ki:* "demon"), whose original Chinese meaning is "soul" or "departed spirit," The left part 云 signifies a cloud and expresses the pronunciation *kon*. The kanji thus represents the idea that the souls of the dead rise up to the clouds. The ancient Japanese pronounced this ideogram *tama*, referring to the life-force energy that enters the body, guiding the heart and mind. Death occurs when the soul (now pronounced *tamashii*) leaves the physical body. In Japan, the word *tamashii* can refer to the soul of either the living or the dead. See also DEMON.

SOUL   *TAMASHII*

夢　夢　夢　夢

The main part of this kanji is made up of 目 for "eye" and 夕 for "night." What is seen in the night are dreams. In Chinese and Japanese, the ideogram for "dream" also has the nuance of "transience" or "fragility." The ancient Chinese legend of "The Kantan Dream" tells of a young man who sets out for the capital to make his fortune, stopping at a small town called Kantan along the way and falling asleep at a station house. As he sleeps, he dreams of becoming the king in the capital. In his dream, he has become old, very sick, and near death. When he awakens, he realizes that he has dreamed his whole life away. Now aware that life is fleeting, he returns to his hometown, where he spends the rest of his life living humbly and satisfied.

DREAM   *YUME*

愛　愛　愛　愛

At the center of this kanji is 心, the ideogram for "heart." Above the heart is the kanji for "breath," and below the heart is the kanji for "graceful movement." Love breathes mercy into the heart, bringing grace into the body and transforming us. This ideogram was originally made of 心 plus 旡, which meant "feeding a guest." The original Chinese meaning was more "hospitality of the heart," or "to show mercy." In Japan, the kanji was first used to express the feeling of liking, admiring, and appreciating things like nature or art, but when Christianity arrived in the middle of the nineteenth century, 愛 (ai) began to take on the European meaning of "love." See also HEART.

LOVE *AI*

精神
精神
精神
精神

This word combines 精 (*sei*), meaning "pure," "superior," or "profound," with 神 (*shin*), meaning "mind" or "soul." The 米 radical on the left side of 精 means "rice"; its original meaning was "polished rice becomes pure." The kanji 神 combines 示, which symbolizes god or the divine, and 申, which originally symbolized a thunderbolt and later meant "to give orders." Chinese mythology says that we enter the world and receive our soul at birth, which becomes an active "spirit" (*shen*) at death. It is believed that these spirits send us "signs" from the netherworld to guide us in life.

精神

SPIRIT   *SEI-SHIN*

The Animals

of the Twelve Zodiac Signs

Around 2000 B.C., the ancient Chinese discovered that Jupiter—which they considered the most auspicious planet—orbited the earth every twelve years. The Chinese astronomers divided the orbit into twelve directions and gave each direction a different name. These names were used merely to indicate the year and Jupiter's position, like the points on a compass. Later, around 100 B.C., the name of an animal was assigned to each of the twelve directions, perhaps to help people remember their birth years. Over time, persons born in a particular year were thought to possess qualities of that year's animal, a belief that continues to this day. The cycle of twelve animals begins again every twelve years. Each year is represented by two kanji, and both are listed here: the first is a kunyomi reading for the animal assigned to the year, and the second is an onyomi reading for the original Chinese name or "compass point."

nezumi

RAT   The top symbolizes its head and teeth. In Japan, the white rat is considered a messenger of the God of Wealth, Daikokuten, harbinger of prosperity and success.

shi, ne

YEAR OF THE RAT   *North.* The original Chinese ideogram symbolizes a seed from which everything on earth is born. The end of something is the beginning of something else.

ushi

OX   In Asia, the ox and cow are used for cultivation and transporting goods. Their hardworking nature epitomizes patience and perseverance.

chū, ushi

YEAR OF THE OX   *North-northeast.* The original Chinese ideogram depicts a root with a seed emerging from it. Those born in this year are patient and steadfast and inspire confidence in others.

tora

TIGER   The kanji depicts an open mouth, roaring. There were no lions in Asia, so the tiger was considered the strongest animal in the jungle.

in, tora

YEAR OF THE TIGER   *East-northeast.* The tiger represents a prudent person, and those born in this year are fierce and can be rebellious, but also courageous, sensitive, deep-thinking, and sympathetic.

usagi

RABBIT   The curved line at the top symbolizes its ears. Japanese believe a rabbit makes rice cakes on the moon, a belief dating back to an old Indian legend.

bō, u

YEAR OF THE RABBIT   *East.* The original Chinese ideogram depicts a plant that has begun to grow. Those born in this year are articulate, talented, and ambitious. They are virtuous and admired by others.

龍
ryū

DRAGON The kanji is a profile of a dragon. The Japanese believe the dragon causes rain and thunder, thus a cyclone is a "coiled dragon" or *tatsumaki*.

辰
shin, tatsu

YEAR OF THE DRAGON *East-southeast.* The original Chinese ideogram symbolizes growth to maturity in spring. Those born this year are energetic, excitable, brave, and honest.

蛇
hebi

SNAKE The element on the left meant a large-headed snake but later became the character for "insect." The snake is considered a messenger of the gods.

巳
shi, mi

YEAR OF THE SNAKE *South-southeast.* The original Chinese ideogram symbolizes the time of year when the day is longest. Those born in this year are outwardly calm but inwardly fiery and passionate.

馬
uma

HORSE The kanji depicts a galloping horse. The custom of bringing a horse to a shrine lives on in wish-placards called 絵馬 (*ema*), "horse pictures."

午
go, uma

YEAR OF THE HORSE *South.* The original Chinese ideogram expresses the balance of light and dark forces. Those born in this year are fast-paced, cheerful, popular, perceptive, and dexterous.

羊
hitsuji

SHEEP/RAM A sheep, with two spikes representing the horns. Sheep were docile and used for sacrifices, so this ideogram also means "goodness."

未
mi, hitsuji

YEAR OF THE RAM *South-southwest.* The original Chinese ideogram shows leaves and branches from a stem. Those born in this year are gentle and compassionate, often shy but elegant and artistic.

猿
saru

MONKEY Monkeys are messengers of god and protective spirits. Samurai used to keep them in their stables to shield their horses from evil.

申
shin, saru

YEAR OF THE MONKEY *West-southwest.* The original Chinese ideogram means "maturing in autumn." Those born this year are inventive, skillful, and strong willed. The Chinese consider them "erratic geniuses."

鷄
niwatori

ROOSTER The element on the right depicts a bird with long feathers. Roosters were kept on temple grounds because they woke up the priests in time for rituals.

酉
yū, tori

YEAR OF THE COCK/ROOSTER *West.* The original Chinese ideogram depicts a bottle of spirits. Those born this year are deep-thinking, capable, and outspoken, preferring to stay busy and socialize.

犬
inu

DOG The kanji depicts a walking dog, with a prominent ear. Dogs are revered in Japan for their loyalty, like Tokyo's famous Hachiko that awaited its long-dead master.

戌
jutsu, inu

YEAR OF THE DOG *West-northwest.* The original ideogram symbolizes the time when leaves and grass wither. Those born in this year have a strong sense of justice, honesty, privacy, honor, and loyalty.

猪
inoshishi

WILD BOAR Buddhism proscribed the eating of meat, but Japanese continued to hunt wild boar. Pork is now consumed in Japan, and the kanji 豚 (*buta*) is used for "pig."

亥
gai, i

YEAR OF THE PIG *North-northwest.* The original Chinese ideogram means "core" or "center." Those born in this year are strong-willed, chivalrous, and enjoy learning.

BIBLIOGRAPHY

The following references were consulted in the preparation of this book:

Bukkyōjiten (Buddhism Dictionary). Tokyo: Iwanami Shoten, 2002.

Chūgoku no Shisō (Chinese Thought). Tokyo: Tokuma Shoten, 1973.

Fukutake Kanwajiten (Fukutake Kanji Dictionary). Tokyo: Fukutake Shoten, 1987.

Iwanami Kokugojiten (Iwanami Japanese Dictionary). Tokyo: Iwanami Shoten, 1974.

Kamo-no-Chōmei, *Hojoki: Visions of a Torn World*. Translated by Yasuhiko Moriguchi and David Jenkins. Berkeley: Stone Bridge Press, 1996.

Kanno, Michiaki. *Jigen* (The Origin of Kanji). Tokyo: Kadokawa Shoten, 1962.

Kogojiten (Archaic Japanese Words Dictionary). Tokyo: Kadokawa Shoten, 1974.

Kojien (Kojien Japanese Dictionary). Tokyo: Iwanami Shoten, 1998.

Minakata Kumakusu Senshū (Selected Works of Kumakusu Minakata). Tokyo: Heibon Sha, 1984.

Nihon Shijin Zenshū (Collected Works of Japanese Poets). Tokyo: Shinchō Sha, 1973.

Sekai no Meicho (World Classic Books). Tokyo: Chuōkōron Sha, 1968.

Shinchō Koten Shūsei (Collected Series of Japanese Classics). Tokyo: Shinchō Sha, 1982.

Shinsen Kanwajiten (New Selected Kanji Dictionary). Tokyo: Shōgakukan, 1970.

Shirakawa, Shizuka. *Jitō* (The Kanji Dictionary). Tokyo: Heibon Sha, 1994.

Yanagida Kunio Zenshū (Collected Works of Kunio Yanagida). Tokyo: Chikuma Shobō, 1990.

A few online kanji resources are:

www.123rf.com/stock-photo/kanji.html: stock kanji images for reproduction

www.c-c-c.org/menu-resources/zodiac: Chinese Culture Center of San Francisco's Zodiac page

www.Japan-Guide.com: resources on Japan

www.joyokanji.com: Eve Kushner's "Joy o' Kanji," featuring essays and photos on kanji and kanji-related subjects

Two recommended books for kanji students are:

Henshall, Kenneth. *A Guide to Remembering Japanese Characters*. Tokyo: Tuttle, 1995.

Rowley, Michael. *Kanji Pict-o-Graphix: Over 1,000 Japanese Kanji and Kana Mnemonics*. Berkeley: Stone Bridge Press, 1992.

INDEX

Printed in the USA
CPSIA information can be obtained
at www.ICGtesting.com
JSHW012054140824
68134JS00035B/3436